Do You Like Getting Creative?

Diane Lindsey Reeves

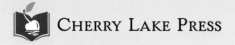
CHERRY LAKE PRESS

Published in the United States of America by Cherry Lake Publishing Group
Ann Arbor, Michigan
www.cherrylakepublishing.com

Reading Adviser: Beth Walker Gambro, MS, Ed., Reading Consultant, Yorkville, IL

Photo Credits: cover: © LightField Studios/Shutterstock; page 5: © nodff/Shutterstock; page 6: © Richard Thornton/ Shutterstock; page 7: © SeventyFour/Shutterstock; page 8: © Halfpoint/Shutterstock; page 9: © Monkey Business Images/Shutterstock; page 10: © wee dezign/Shutterstock; page 11: © Rawpixel.com/Shutterstock; page 12: © Unai Huizi Photography/Shutterstock; page 13: © Africa Studio/Shutterstock; page 14: © Ground Picture/Shutterstock; page 15: © rCarner/Shutterstock; page 16: © Zamrznuti tonovi/Shutterstock; page 17: © Tatyana Soares/Shutterstock; page 18: © YAKOBCHUK VIACHESLAV/Shutterstock; page 19: © Kostikova Natalia/Shutterstock; page 20: © Stokkete/ Shutterstock; page 21: © Milan Ilic Photographer/Shutterstock; page 22: © Friends Stock/Shutterstock; page 23: © Dragon Images/Shutterstock; page 24: © Pixel-Shot/Shutterstock; page 25: © DC Studio/Shutterstock; page 26: © Kaspars Grinvalds/Shutterstock; page 27: © REDPIXEL.PL/Shutterstock; page 30: © Laugesen Mateo/Shutterstock; page 31: © CREATISTA/Shutterstock

Cherry Lake Press is an imprint of Cherry Lake Publishing Group.

Library of Congress Cataloging-in-Publication Data

Names: Reeves, Diane Lindsey, 1959- author.
Title: Do you like getting creative? / by Diane Lindsey Reeves.
Description: Ann Arbor, Michigan : Cherry Lake Publishing, [2023] | Series: Career clues for kids | Audience: Grades 4-6
Summary: "Would you consider yourself creative? That might be a potential clue to your future career! This book explores what a career in art might look like. Readers will discover how their interests can lead to a lifelong future career. Aligned to curriculum standards and 21st Century Skills, Career Clues for Kids prepares readers for a successful future. Includes table of contents, glossary, index, sidebars, and author biographies"— Provided by publisher.
Identifiers: LCCN 2022039262 | ISBN 9781668919460 (hardcover) | ISBN 9781668920480 (paperback) | ISBN 9781668923146 (pdf) | ISBN 9781668921814 (ebook)
Subjects: LCSH: Cultural industries—Vocational guidance—Juvenile literature. | Arts—Vocational guidance— Juvenile literature.
Classification: LCC HD9999.C9472 R44 2023 | DDC 338.4/77023—dc23/eng/20221020
LC record available at https://lccn.loc.gov/2022039262

Cherry Lake Publishing Group would like to acknowledge the work of the Partnership for 21st Century Learning, a Network of Battelle for Kids. Please visit *http://www.battelleforkids.org/networks/p21* for more information.

Printed in the United States of America
Corporate Graphics

Diane Lindsey Reeves likes to write books that help students figure out what they want to be when they grow up. She mostly lives in Washington, D.C., but spends as much time as she can in North Carolina and South Carolina with her grandkids.

CONTENTS

Creating a Cool Career

Figuring out what you want to be when you grow up can be tricky. There are so many choices! How are you supposed to know which one to pick? Here's an idea... follow the clues!

The fact that you are reading a book called *Do You Like Getting Creative?* is your first clue. It suggests that you have an interest in art, music, and other creative things. True? If so, start looking at different careers where you can create a cool future!

Your **interests** say a lot about who you are and what makes you tick. What do you like doing best?

Abilities are things that you are naturally good at doing. Another word for ability is talent. Everyone has natural talents and abilities. Some are more obvious than others. What are you really good at doing?

Curiosity offers up other career clues. To succeed in any career, you have to learn what it takes to do that job. You may have to go to college or trade school. It may take gaining new skills and getting experience. Curiosity about a subject keeps you at it until you are an expert. What do you want to know more about?

Interests. Abilities. Curiosity. These clues can help you find a career that's right for you.

FIND THE CLUES!

Each chapter includes several clues about careers you might enjoy.

INTERESTS: **What do you like doing?**

ABILITIES: **What are you good at doing?**

CURIOSITY: **What do you want to learn more about?**

Are You a Future Creator?

WOULD YOU ENJOY...

Teaching other people how to get creative? (see page 8)

Working with creative teams to make TV ads? (see page 10)

Helping other people look their best? (see page 12)

Making anything with words sound good? (page 14)

Making art with flowers? (see page 16)

Decorating houses and businesses? (see page 18)

Entertaining people with music? (see page 20)

Running the sound board at concerts and plays? (see page 22)

Playing video games for a living? (see page 24)

Creating new places to surf on the web? (see page 26)

READ ON FOR MORE CLUES ABOUT CREATIVE CAREERS!

Arts Teacher

A person who instructs others about art, drama, dance, or music.

Can you act, sing, play an instrument, or create art? Be sure to thank your arts teacher! Arts teachers share what they know about their favorite art form. They work with students of all ages. Most focus on a specific type of art. Drama teachers teach performance arts. Music teachers teach choral groups and bands. Art teachers teach art history, painting, drawing, pottery, and more. Can you guess what dance teachers teach? Arts are an important part of learning for everyone. It unlocks creativity and powers imagination.

CLUES!

INTEREST: Moving and grooving in creative ways

ABILITY: Teaching others new skills

CURIOSITY: Sharing artistic talents with others

INVESTIGATE!

NOW: Get involved in the school band, drama club, or arts program.

LATER: Earn a college degree in music, drama, or art.

Art Director

A person who oversees an ad or media campaign.

Have you seen any good commercials lately? TV ads involve lots of creative people doing lots of creative jobs. So do magazine ads and media campaigns. An art director brings all that creative energy together. It starts with a client who wants to sell more products. Let's say there's a fast food chain that wants to sell more kids' meals. The art director plans out TV commercials, print ads, and **social media**. A creative team includes writers, actors, designers, and others. They work together to create memorable ways to get the word out. They'll know they've succeeded when more people buy those kids' meals!

CLUES!

INTEREST: Watching funny TV commercials and online **memes**

ABILITY: Making posters to promote school events

CURIOSITY: Creative leadership skills

INVESTIGATE!

NOW: Have fun making up commercials with friends.

LATER: Earn a college degree in art or design.

Cosmetologist

A person who provides beauty services for hair, nails, and skin.

Cosmetologist is the fancy name for hair stylists, makeup artists, and nail techs. Their job is to keep people looking good. Hair stylists work in hair salons and barber shops. They cut, style, color, and treat hair for men, women, and kids. Finding the right look for each client is their number one goal. Makeup artists work in hair salons. They also work in retail stores. Some even work in Hollywood doing makeup for the stars! Nail techs pamper clients with **manicures** and **pedicures**. They work in nail salons.

CLUES!

INTEREST: Following the latest trends in hair and make-up

ABILITY: Trying out new looks

CURIOSITY: The art of looking good

INVESTIGATE!

NOW: Practice trading manicures with friends.

LATER: Complete a cosmetology training program or apprenticeship.

Editor

A person who edits writing before it is published.

Have you ever heard the saying "all good writing is rewriting"? Teachers say it a lot to get students to edit their work. Editors make a living editing the work of authors. Sure, they fix grammar and spelling mistakes. But there's more to it than that. They work with authors to come up with ideas. They suggest ways to make a good book even better. Many editors edit fiction or nonfiction books for children or adults. Others edit online content or work for companies that create technical documents.

CLUES!

INTEREST: Reading good books

ABILITY: Writing stories and school reports

CURIOSITY: How publishing works

INVESTIGATE!

NOW: Get involved with your school newspaper or yearbook club.

LATER: Earn a college degree in English, communications, or journalism.

Floral Designer

A person who creates arrangements using plant materials and flowers.

Floral designers are there for people on their best and worst days. Their work celebrates big events like weddings and holidays. It also provides comfort for funerals or when someone is ill. Floral designers use flowers to create art. They are creative. They are experts in flowers and other green growing things. In some cases, they also run their own shops. Deadlines are a big deal for floral designers. No one wants to get a bridal bouquet the day *after* their wedding! Knowing how to talk ideas with customers is another helpful skill.

CLUES!

INTEREST: **Flowers and color**

ABILITY: **Growing things**

CURIOSITY: **The art of flowers**

INVESTIGATE!

NOW: **Gather flowers and greenery from outside to decorate your family's dinner table.**

LATER: **Get experience in a floral shop or find training at a community college.**

Interior Designer

A person who decorates people's houses and businesses.

What's your decorating style? Do you like modern or cozy? Lots of color or neutral tones? Interior designers ask their clients questions like these. You probably know that interior designers decorate people's homes. But did you know they also decorate hotels, spas, churches, schools, restaurants, and even cruise ships and airplanes? They must pay careful attention to each client's taste and the purpose of the space. They have many details to consider. Paint colors, carpet, furniture, and artwork all make the list. Be sure to measure the decorating space! Then measure it again.

CLUES!

INTEREST: Watching home shows on TV

ABILITY: Decorating your bedroom or locker

CURIOSITY: How to design beautiful spaces

INVESTIGATE!

NOW: Use pictures from magazines or websites to sketch out plans for your dream bedroom.

LATER: Earn at least a 2-year associate degree in interior design.

Musician

A person who sings, plays, or writes music.

A career as a musician means different things to different people. It can involve vocals or instruments. It might involve the opera, a jazz band, or performing in a Broadway play. Some musicians become rock stars. Others compose hit songs. Still others conduct orchestras or teach. No matter which path they take, all musicians have three things in common. One is musical talent. Another is a lifetime of practice. And most of all, they share a love of music. That's what keeps them at it when rehearsals go long!

CLUES!

INTEREST: Listening to and playing music

ABILITY: Entertaining people with music

CURIOSITY: How to sing or play an instrument even better that you can now

INVESTIGATE!

NOW: Join the school band or chorus.

LATER: Earn a college degree in music.

Sound Engineer

A person who produces live or recorded performances.

Music is meant to be heard. Sound engineers make that happen at concerts and in recording studios. They operate high-tech digital work stations to capture the sounds that voices and instruments make in just the right way. They use equipment to amplify, enhance, record, or mix sound in all kinds of recording situations. Have you ever seen the cockpit of an airplane? A sound engineer's control room is similar. It has an amazing number of levers and gadgets to control.

CLUES!

INTEREST: **Running the sound equipment at a school sporting event or worship service**

ABILITY: **Staying cool, calm, and collected**

CURIOSITY: **Using technology to improve the sound of music**

INVESTIGATE!

NOW: **Use a smartphone or tablet to record sounds around the house.**

LATER: **Apprenticeship and on-the-job training or college degree in audio engineering.**

Video Game Designer

A person who makes video game content and action come alive.

Getting paid to make video games sounds like a dream come true for many gamers. By most accounts, it is a pretty cool job. However, there is a lot more to it than playing games. Video game designers are part of a team that creates ideas for video games. They help create the characters, setting, rules, and story. On the technical side, they use special **animation** software to create each scene. Some even write the code that drives all the online action. The process is complex and takes lots of time. But when the job is done right—wow!

CLUES!

INTERESTS: Video gaming

ABILITIES: Reaching the highest levels of your favorite games

CURIOSITY: How to turn fun ideas into popular video games

INVESTIGATE!

NOW: Play video games—after you finish your homework, of course.

LATER: Earn a 2- or 4-year college degree in digital arts or animation.

Webmaster

A person who creates and maintains websites.

Webmasters create websites for the Internet. The job has three parts. One part is computer coding. Webmasters use HTML coding and scripting languages to set up pages for online viewing. Another part is graphic design. That's where they use creative skills to make the website look good. The third part is organization. They set up navigation systems to make information easy to find. Businesses with e-commerce sites often use webmasters to set up and run their online storefronts.

CLUES!

INTERESTS: Surfing the web with an adult's supervision

ABILITIES: Using computer design tools

CURIOSITY: How websites work

INVESTIGATE!

NOW: Make storyboards for a cool website you'd like to create.

LATER: Online training or associate degree in web design.

Creative Workshop

Keep investigating those career clues until you find a career that's right for you! Here are more ways to explore.

Join a Club

Get involved in your school's drama club, art club, band, chorus and other in-school and after-school arts programs.

Talk to People with Interesting Careers

Ask your teacher or parent to help you connect with someone who has a career like the one you want. Be ready to ask lots of questions!

Volunteer

Look for opportunities to help out at art camps at your local community center.

Enjoy Career Day

School career days can be a great way to find out more about different careers. Make the most of this opportunity.

Explore Online

With adult supervision, use your favorite search engine to look online for information about careers you are interested in.

Participate in Take Your Daughters and Sons to Work Day

Every year on the fourth Thursday of April, kids all over the world go to work with their parents or other trusted adults to find out what the world of work is really like.

Find out more at: https://daughtersandsonstowork.org

Resources

Art Director
My Next Move: Art Director
https://www.mynextmove.org/profile/summary/27-1011.00

Arts Teacher
Metropolitan Museum of Art: MetKids
*https://www.metmuseum.org/art/online-features/
metkids/explore*

Cosmetologist
Anton, Carrie. *The Skin & Nails Book.* Middleton, WI:
American Girl Publishing, 2018.

Editor
Scribblitt
https://www.scribblitt.com

Floral Designer
Jose, Sarah. *Trees, Leaves, Flowers and Seeds: A Visual
Encyclopedia of the Plant Kingdom.* New York, NY:
DK Publishing, 2019.

Interior Designer
HGTV: Kid's Rooms
https://www.hgtv.com/design/rooms/kid-rooms

Musician
KidSearch: Live Free Streaming Kids Safe Radio
http://www.kidzsearch.com/radio.html

Sound Engineer
YouTube: What Does a Sound Engineer Do?
https://www.youtube.com/watch?v=S9WnYUUBl84

Video Game Designer
Scratch
https://scratch.mit.edu

Webmaster
Verywell Family: Fun and Free Educational Websites for Kids
https://www.verywellfamily.com/best-free-educational-websites-for-kids-3129084

Glossary

abilities (uh-BIH-luh-teez) natural talents or acquired skills

animation (aa-nuh-MAY-shuhn) making movies by using pictures, drawings, or computer graphics

apprenticeship (uh-PREHN-tuh-ship) a way to learn a trade by working under someone with skills and experience in that trade

curiosity (kyur-ee-AH-suh-tee) strong desire to know or learn about something

interests (IN-tuh-ruhsts) things or activities that a person enjoys or is concerned about

manicure (MAH-nuh-kyoor) cleaning, shaping, and polishing of fingernails

meme (MEEM) funny or interesting item, such as a picture or video, that is spread widely online

pedicure (PEH-duh-kyoor) cleaning, shaping, and polishing of toenails

social media (SO-shul MEE-dee-uh) forms of communication that let people share information using the internet or smartphones

Index